CW01238322

PUFFIN BOOKS

UK | USA | Canada | Ireland | Australia
India | New Zealand | South Africa

Puffin Books is part of the Penguin Random House group of companies whose addresses can be found at global.penguinrandomhouse.com.

www.penguin.co.uk
www.puffin.co.uk
www.ladybird.co.uk

Penguin Random House UK

First published 2020

001

Text copyright © Michael Lee Richardson, 2020
Illustrations copyright © Freda Chiu, 2020

Unpublished writings of A. M. Turing © The Provost and Scholars of Kings College Cambridge, 2020

The moral right of the author and illustrator has been asserted

Text design by Perfect Bound Ltd
Printed and bound in Great Britain by Clays Ltd, Elcograf S.p.A.

A CIP catalogue record for this book is available from the British Library

ISBN: 978-0-241-43401-7

All correspondence to:
Puffin Books
Penguin Random House Children's
One Embassy Gardens, New Union Square
5 Nine Elms Lane, London SW8 5DA

MIX
Paper from responsible sources
FSC® C018179

Penguin Random House is committed to a sustainable future for our business, our readers and our planet. This book is made from Forest Stewardship Council® certified paper.

THE EXTRAORDINARY LIFE OF
ALAN TURING

THE EXTRAORDINARY LIFE OF
ALAN TURING

Written by Michael Lee Richardson
Illustrated by Freda Chiu

EXTRAORDINARY LIVES
PUFFIN

Who was Alan Turing?

Alan Mathison Turing

was born in Maida Vale, London,
on 23 June 1912.

Some people call Alan the grandfather of the modern computer because of his invention of the incredible Turing machine. Alan has also gone down in history for his extremely important role in **defeating the Nazis** in the Second World War because of his codebreaking skills.

Alan was known for being **quiet and shy**, and he had a high-pitched voice and a distinctive laugh. His shirts were often untucked, and his hair messy.

Alan showed an early talent for **maths and science**, though he wasn't quite as good at subjects he didn't like. He was bottom of his class in Latin, and his English teacher said his **handwriting** was the worst they had ever seen!

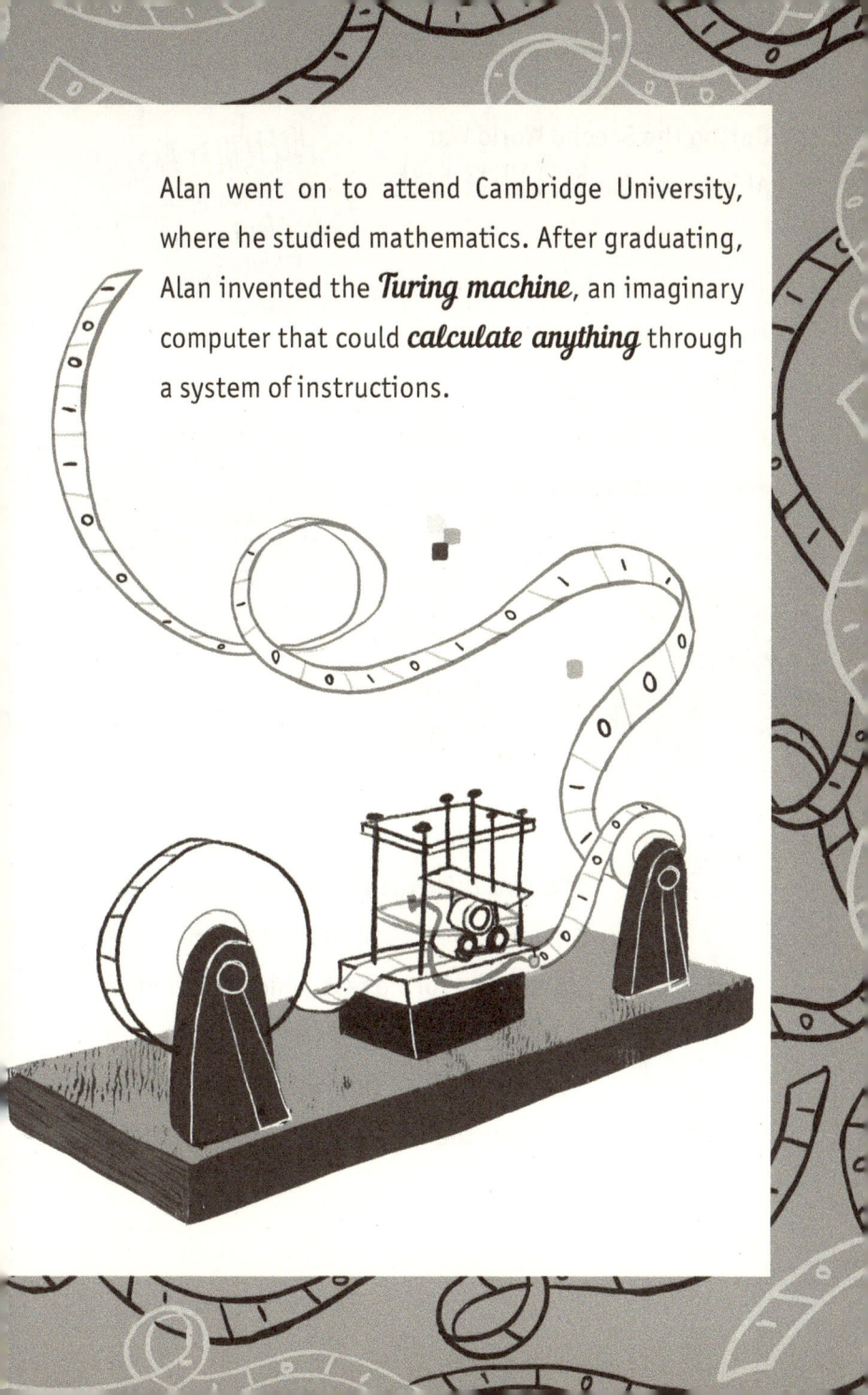

Alan went on to attend Cambridge University, where he studied mathematics. After graduating, Alan invented the *Turing machine*, an imaginary computer that could **calculate anything** through a system of instructions.

During the Second World War Alan worked at BLETCHLEY PARK.

There Alan helped create the *bombe*, an early ELECTROMECHANICAL computer that could decode *secret messages* sent between enemy soldiers during the war. Alan's work was crucial in helping the Allies defeat the Nazis.

After the war Alan turned his attention to *artificial intelligence*, a field so new that it hadn't even been named yet! He came up with the Turing test, which determines a machine's ability to trick someone into believing it is human. This was used when the first *working computers* were created.

BLETCHLEY PARK: a top-secret centre for British codebreakers.

ELECTRO-MECHANICAL: a mechanical device operated by electricity.

'MACHINES take me by SURPRISE with great FREQUENCY.'

Alan was PERSECUTED during his lifetime for being gay.

PERSECUTION: the systematic mistreatment of an individual or a group by another individual or group.

At the time being gay was *illegal*, and when the police found out that Alan had been in a relationship with another man he was arrested and **convicted** as a criminal. He was no longer able to work as a codebreaker.

In 1954 Alan's housekeeper found him dead from cyanide poisoning. Some people believe that Alan had meant to poison himself. Others think it was the result of an experiment gone wrong.

Alan's legacy

Historians believe that Alan's inventions shortened the Second World War by more than two years and saved over fourteen million lives. But due to the top-secret nature of Alan's work, many people didn't find out about it until long after he died.

'We can only see a short distance ahead, but we can see PLENTY there that needs to be done.'

Turing's top inventions

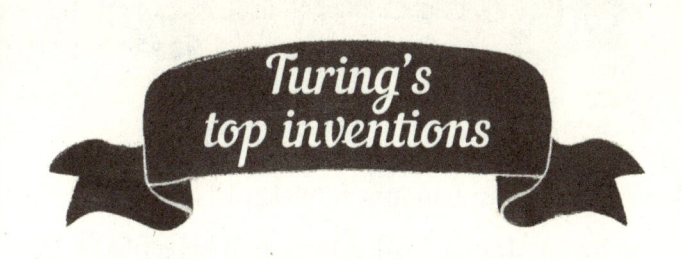

THE TURING MACHINE
– an imaginary system that can calculate anything a modern computer can (which Alan thought of before computers and calculators were even invented!).

THE BOMBE
– a machine used to decode secret messages during the Second World War.

THE TURING TEST
– which determines a machine's ability to trick someone into believing it is human.

Alan's early life

Alan was born in London, in 1912. His father, *Julius*, worked for the Indian civil service and his mother, *Ethel Sara Stoney*, was the daughter of the chief engineer of the Madras railway. Both of his parents spent a lot of time in India when Alan was a child.

When their parents were away Alan and his older brother, *John*, lived with a retired military couple, Colonel and Mrs Ward, in St Leonards-on-Sea, a seaside town near Hastings in East Sussex.

Colonel and Mrs Ward had four daughters of their own, and also took in three of Alan's cousins. It was a good job they had a **large house** with a big nursery!

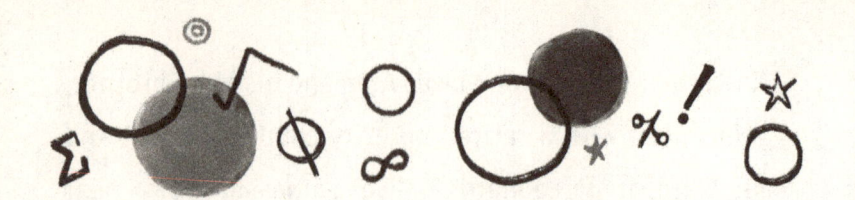

Alan was a curious child, and he was a **stickler for the rules**. Once, when Alan and his nanny were playing a game, his nanny fixed the game so that Alan would win. When Alan realized, he flew into **a tantrum**!

Alan was always asking questions, which some people found rude or cheeky.

Because his parents were away so often, it was John's responsibility to get Alan dressed in the **sailor suits** that were popular at the time – though John would complain that Alan couldn't keep himself clean and tidy for more than five minutes.

Alan and John

Alan taught himself to read in only three weeks, and he was very fond of numbers. When he was out for walks he would stop at every lamppost to check its serial number.

He was especially interested in science and would often do *experiments* of his own. He once planted his broken toy soldiers in the ground to see if he could grow new soldiers from the broken pieces.

Growing up, Alan's favourite hobby was science, and his favourite book was *Natural Wonders Every Child Should Know* by Edwin Tenney Brewster. The book was all about **nature and biology**, and Alan's mother had given it to him as a Christmas present when he was ten.

Alan treasured it throughout his life. It fed what would end up being his lifelong **fascination** with science.

'A very large part of SPACE-TIME must be investigated, if RELIABLE RESULTS are to be OBTAINED.'

Growing up

Although they weren't rich, Julius's job as a civil servant meant that the Turings were thought of as quite a respectable family, and Alan and his brother had everything they needed. When Alan's parents were back from India, the family would enjoy holidays in Scotland and France, and even a trip to Switzerland where Alan learned to ski.

At the time young boys like Alan were expected to go to private school. Here they would learn the skills they would need to SOCIALIZE in British society and were trained for **high-ranking jobs** in the military, business and politics. Alan wanted to be a **doctor** when he grew up.

SOCIALIZE: mix with other people in a way that is acceptable to society.

In order to get a good, 'respectable' job when they were older, boys were expected to pursue a classical education. So at the age of six Alan was sent to St Michael's, a private day school in Hastings, in order to include Latin in his learning. Although he would later show a flair for learning languages, Alan struggled at school.

A classical education included the study of literature, poetry, drama, philosophy, history, art and foreign languages.

Alan later went to Hazelhurst Preparatory School in Sussex. At Hazelhurst Alan became interested in chess, spending hours working out complex chess problems on his own.

'*I have had* CLEVER BOYS AND HARD-WORKING BOYS, *but Alan is* A GENIUS.'

– Miss Taylor, head teacher

Alan didn't have a huge amount of friends, and some people thought of him as lonely.

Alan's mother Ethel (usually called by her middle name Sara) was a **talented artist**. While Alan was at Hazelhurst, Sara drew a picture of Alan that she sent as a gift to the matron at the school. Sara titled the drawing 'Hockey or Watching the Daisies Grow'. It shows a young Alan out on the hockey pitch. While the other boys celebrate their win in the background, Alan examines the flowers in the foreground.

Alan's *passion for science* continued to grow. As well as reading about nature and biology, he would perform simple chemistry *experiments*, and create his own clever inventions.

He still struggled with *messy handwriting*, so he invented his own fountain pen, which he used to write to his mum and dad in India.

Alan's letter to Mr and Mrs Turing in India, 1 April 1923:

Dear Mummy and Daddy,

Guess what I am writing with? It is an invention of my own. It is a fountain pen like this: -

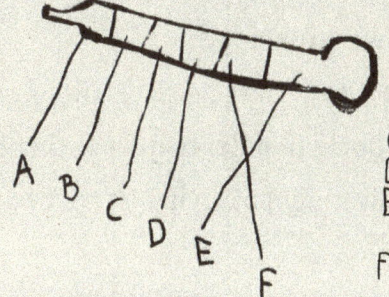

A nib
B cork to stop ink and hold nib
C ink
D tube for ink
E end of fountain pen filler
F air

You see to fill it scweeze E and let go and the ink is sucked up and it is full. I have arranged it so that when I press a little of the ink comes down but it keeps on getting clogged.

Sherborne

When Alan was thirteen, he went to Sherborne, a boarding school in Dorset.

On his very first day at Sherborne there was a GENERAL STRIKE, which meant that none of the trains or buses were running. Alan had to ride his bicycle sixty miles from Southampton Docks in order to get to school, and even stayed overnight at an inn on his own.

GENERAL STRIKE: a strike in May 1926 by workers in many industries in support of coal miners whose pay and working conditions were under threat.

Alan accidentally left his suitcases at the inn, so he had to endure the first week at his new school without any of his *belongings*.

'It's an awful NUISANCE here without any of my clothes or anything. IT'S RATHER HARD getting settled down.'

Alan was put in Westcott House, a boarding house whose colours were black and white. Here Alan lived with nearly fifty other boys.

DID YOU KNOW?
In 2016 Alan's nephew Sir Dermot Turing unveiled a blue plaque outside Westcott House, commemorating Alan's time at Sherborne.

Alan struggled at Sherborne. He still had issues with his handwriting and using a fountain pen. His hands and collar were frequently covered in black and blue *ink spots*. He would often walk around with his shirt untucked or buttoned up wrong, or his school cap on skew-whiff.

Other boys made fun of him for his scruffy appearance and for his hesitant high-pitched voice.

Even his teachers recognized that he didn't quite fit in. His head teacher wrote in his school report in spring 1927:

> *'He would do much better if he would do his best as a member of this school – he should have much more* ESPRIT DE CORPS.'

ESPRIT DE CORPS: a feeling of pride and loyalty shared by members of a group, essentially team spirit.

He continued to pursue his passions for maths and science. At the age of fourteen Alan could solve super-advanced problems. He once calculated the value of pi to thirty-six decimal places – just for fun!

π

What is pi?

Pi, or π, is a mathematical constant that measures the ratio of the distance around a circle – the circumference – to the circle's diameter. When the circumference and the diameter are divided – no matter what the numbers are – the results are always the same. Alan calculated pi to 3.14159265358979323846264338327950 2884. However, he could have kept going, because pi is an infinite decimal – it continues without repeating patterns forever!

For Christmas in 1927 Alan's grandfather gave him a copy of Albert Einstein's *The Theory of Relativity*. Alan filled an entire notebook by putting the arguments of *The Theory of Relativity* into simple form, which he sent to his mother.

The notebook shows that Alan not only understood Einstein's complicated theory, but that he EXTRAPOLATED Einstein's questioning of Newton's laws of motion – which Einstein didn't even write about in the book!

EXTRAPOLATE: draw conclusions about, read between the lines.

Albert Einstein's theory of general relativity explains many subjects from the motion of the planets in the solar system and the existence of black holes to the effect of gravity on light.

Isaac Newton's laws of motion stated that: if an object is still, it will remain still until an external force acts upon it. Force equals mass times acceleration. For every action there is an equal and opposite reaction.

Alan's talent for maths and science didn't earn him the **respect** of some of his teachers at school, who placed more value on subjects like Latin and English. Alan was bottom of his class in English. His Latin teacher wrote in his school report: 'He is ludicrously behind.'

Christopher

In 1928, when Alan was sixteen, Alan entered sixth-form college at Sherborne School, which is where he met his ***best friend***, Christopher Morcom.

Christopher was almost a year older than Alan. He was a member of Lyon House at Sherborne, whose colours were blue and black.

DID YOU KNOW?

Christopher had a wicked sense of humour and was known for pulling pranks. He once got into trouble for sending gas-filled balloons across the field to a nearby girls' school!

'It never seems to have occurred to me to make other friends besides Morcom, he made everyone else seem so ordinary.'

Alan and Christopher were very *different*. Alan was sometimes seen as sloppy and careless, while Christopher was known for being careful and *methodical*.

Despite their differences, their shared enthusiasm for science and maths brought Alan and Christopher together, and the two of them became *inseparable*. Alan and Christopher would meet every Wednesday in the school library to discuss their research. Christopher helped Alan to become more methodical, and he also introduced Alan to ASTRONOMY.

ASTRONOMY: the study of the stars, planets and space.

In December 1929 Alan and Christopher visited Cambridge together so that they could both sit their exams to get into Cambridge University. Alan was just as *excited* about spending the week in Cambridge with Christopher as he was about seeing the famous university city. Many people believe that by this time Alan had fallen in love with Christopher.

Christopher won a scholarship to study maths at Trinity College, Cambridge. Alan didn't.

And then tragedy struck.

Christopher died suddenly in February 1930 of *tuberculosis* before he could take up his place. Alan was devastated. He poured himself into studying science and maths, the subjects he had shared with Christopher, and set about securing a scholarship to Cambridge, just as Christopher had.

After Christopher died Alan began to write to Christopher's mother.

Alan's letter to Frances Isobel Morcom, 15 February 1930, two days after Christopher's death:

> Dear Mrs Morcom,
>
> I want to say how sorry I am about Chris. During the last year I worked with him continually and I am sure I could not have found anywhere another companion so brilliant and yet so charming and unconceited. I regarded my interest in my work, and in such things as astronomy (to which he introduced me) as something to be shared with him and I think he felt a little the same about me. Although that interest is partly gone, I know I must put as much energy, if not as much interest, into my work as if he were alive, because that is what he would like me to do. I feel sure that you could not possibly have had a greater loss.
>
> Yours sincerely,
> Alan Turing

Alan and Mrs Morcom would send each other Christmas cards as well as letters around the times of Christopher's birthday and his death.

Christopher's father, Colonel R. K. Morcom, set up a *prize in his honour* to encourage the pursuit of science among pupils at Christopher's school. Alan won the **Christopher Morcom Prize** in 1930 and 1931.

'I FEEL SURE *that I shall meet* CHRISTOPHER AGAIN SOMEWHERE *and that there will be some work for us to do* TOGETHER . . . *Now that I am left to do it alone I must not let him down.*'

Did You Know?

Some writers and historians have suggested that Alan had many traits common to Asperger's syndrome, a form of autism. These traits include his particular interest in science and maths, his frustration when people weren't following the rules, and his close relationships with only a few people, such as Christopher Morcom. It's impossible to know whether someone has or had autism without a trained professional meeting with them; however, had Alan known what those traits meant and how to get support for them, he may have found life easier and been happier, especially at school.

Life at Cambridge

Alan went on to study mathematics at King's College, Cambridge.

Alan **thrived** at university. He was able to focus on the things he was passionate about, and he no longer had to study things he wasn't interested in. He was still known for being quite unusual, though.

'To call him ODD is perhaps wrong, but unusual, certainly. He was so very LIVELY, so very amusing, and his ideas were always BUBBLING ABOUT.'

– Dr Norman Routledge, one of Alan's friends from Cambridge

As well as maths, Alan enjoyed rowing, running and sailing. He also joined the anti-war movement, which would help organize strikes among munitions factories and chemical workers in countries where governments intended to go to war, and made frequent trips abroad.

Although being gay was illegal at the time, the culture at Cambridge was much more accepting, and Alan was able to embrace his identity as a gay man. His first boyfriend was fellow mathematician *James Atkins*.

While he was at King's College, Alan came up with the idea for the *Turing machine*.

The Turing machine

The Turing machine is an idea of what a machine could do. It can **calculate anything a computer can** – which is all the more remarkable because Alan thought of it long before computers or calculators!

The theoretical machine would be made up of a long series of little boxes, each with a single symbol written in it, such as a number or letter. A tape would feed into the machine, which would then move along the tape, *reading the symbol* in each box. It would start with a set of rules for what action to do when it reads each symbol.

The actions it can do when it reads a symbol:
- write a new symbol in the current box or make the current box blank
- move on to the next box or back to the previous box.

Because it wasn't a real machine, and the imaginary tape and list of symbols could be as long as they needed to be, the model that Alan came up with could compute anything that a computer can, for example, the millionth digit of pi, or the best move to make in a game of chess.

Such imaginary machines allow us to find out what is **_theoretically_** possible or impossible. Alan's invention was a huge **_breakthrough_** for computer science and is still studied to this day. But Alan's greatest invention was yet to come.

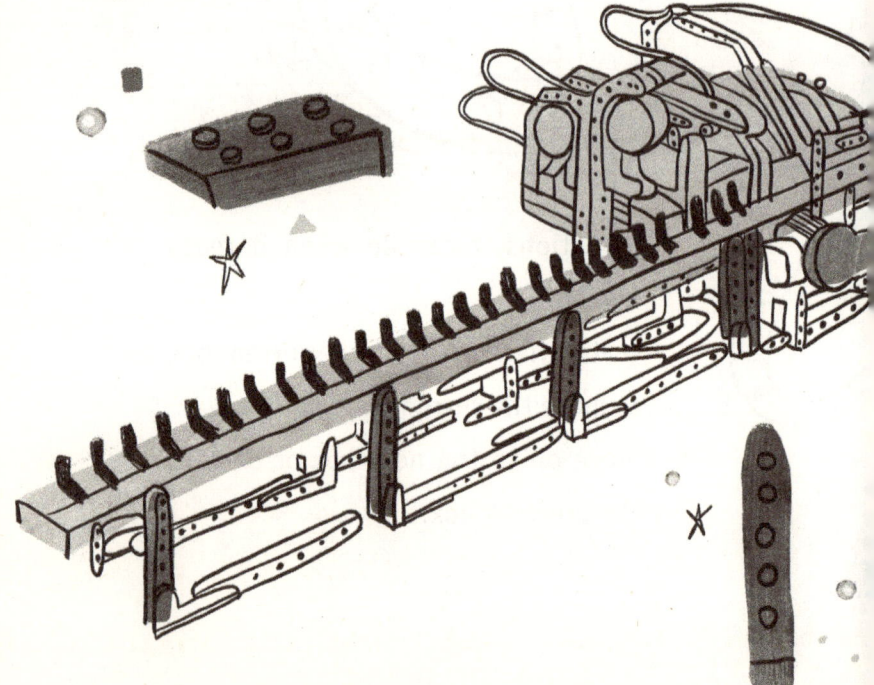

Did You Know?

When Alan designed the Turing machine he never meant for it to be built in real life - however, many people have built functioning Turing machines over the years. To celebrate what would have been Alan's hundredth birthday three Dutch researchers - Davy Landman, Jeroen van den Bos and Paul Klint - even built a functioning Turing machine out of Lego!

'A man provided with **PAPER, PENCIL AND RUBBER,** and subject to **STRICT DISCIPLINE,** is in effect a **UNIVERSAL MACHINE.**'

Graduation

Alan graduated from King's College, Cambridge, in 1934 with top marks. To celebrate he took a trip to Germany with his friend Denis Williams. They took their bicycles to Cologne and cycled almost thirty miles a day.

> Alan and Denis happened to be in Germany during what would later become known as the Night of the Long Knives, when the Nazi regime – led by Adolf Hitler – murdered almost a hundred people for political reasons. The events of that night would eventually lead to the Second World War.

Alan – who had learned German by reading German maths textbooks – translated the story of the Night of the Long Knives from the newspaper for Denis from the comfort and safety of their youth hostel in Hanover.

When he was only twenty-two, Alan became one of the youngest Fellows of King's College, Cambridge. Alan also took a job working with undergraduate students (students who haven't yet completed a degree).

Fellows of King's College were given £300 a month, were able to stay overnight at the university and dine at the High Table whenever they wanted.

Did You Know?

For Christmas in 1934, when he was twenty-two, Alan asked for a teddy bear, because he had never had one as a child. He named the bear Porgy. While he was a Fellow at Cambridge he would often place the bear around his room, so when undergraduates came to him for supervision, for example, they might find Porgy sitting by the fire, reading a book, to which Alan would joke, 'Porgy is very studious this morning.'

Alan later went to Princeton University in New Jersey in the United States for a couple of years where he learned about cryptology, the study of secret communications. It was his knowledge of **cryptology** and **codebreaking** that would go on to make him one of the most important people in the Second World War.

· *New Jersey*

'I am speaking to you from the cabinet room at 10 Downing Street. This morning the British ambassador in Berlin handed the German government a final note stating that unless we heard from them by eleven o'clock that they were prepared at once to withdraw their troops from Poland a state of war would exist between us. I have to tell you now that no such undertaking has been received, and that consequently this country is at war with Germany.'

– British prime minister Neville Chamberlain declares war on Germany

Breaking codes

On 3 September 1939 the British prime minister declared war on Germany.

The next day, Alan reported to Bletchley Park, an old country house in a small town halfway between Oxford and Cambridge.

Bletchley Park was soon to become a top-secret centre for codebreaking, and was known during the war as **Station X**. Station X consisted of a large house surrounded by various wooden huts and brick blocks.

DID YOU KNOW?
About ten thousand people worked in and around Bletchley Park. Around seven thousand of them were women.

Alan worked in Hut 8, where he and his colleagues were tasked with cracking the Enigma code.

The Enigma machine

During the war German soldiers would send secret messages to each other using an Enigma machine. The machine – which looked a bit like an old-fashioned typewriter – was used to scramble and encrypt written messages, so that someone would have to have a special code to decrypt the message and read what it said. The special codes were changed daily and kept secret.

DID YOU KNOW?
There are approximately 150,000,000,000,000 – one hundred and fifty million million! – ways to set an Enigma machine.

The team at Bletchley Park would have to work tirelessly around the clock to crack each day's code. But then Alan and his team came up with a ***brilliant idea***.

The bombe

By studying the Enigma machine Alan and his team worked out, most importantly, that a letter couldn't be encoded as itself. For example, an 'A' couldn't be coded as an 'A' and a 'T' couldn't be coded as a 'T'.

Using designs for a machine that had been created by codebreakers in Poland, Alan and his team took **advantage** of this flaw and invented the bombe, a very early computer. These huge electromechanical devices worked like thirty-six Enigma machines wired together.

Codebreakers would feed parts of an encrypted message into the bombe and the computer would try out different combinations of Enigma settings.

DID YOU KNOW?
The first working bombe was codenamed Victory, and the second Agnus Dei – which the codebreakers at Bletchley Park nicknamed Agnes!

If a setting led to a letter being coded as itself – an 'A' being coded as an 'A' or a 'T' being coded as a 'T' – they would know that combination wasn't right. Then the machine would try another combination.

The bombes were mostly operated by officers from the WRNS – the Women's Royal Naval Service – who were popularly known as Wrens.

Even though it was slow compared to a modern computer, it was much faster than trying to work out the codes by hand. The bombes were used to narrow down the number of possible Enigma settings. Human codebreakers would then look for things like common **German words** in fragments of decoded text.

Once the code was cracked, the workers at Bletchley Park could set up an Enigma machine with the **correct key** and reverse the code for every message intercepted on that day.

DID YOU KNOW?
Each bombe was 1.8 metres tall and 2.1 metres wide, weighing about a ton. They used more than 19 kilometres of wiring and had 97,000 different parts.

The bombes today

Of all the original bombes Alan and his team would have worked with, not a single one exists today. Computer engineer John Harper and his team at the Computer Conservation Society spent thirteen years rebuilding a bombe from Alan and his team's designs. The rebuilt bombe is now on display at Bletchley Park Museum. Audrey Wind, a former Wren and bombe operator, said that the rebuilt bombe isn't quite as noisy as the original – however, she would have been used to multiple bombes in operation at once!

Cracking the code

$\mathcal{E}$arly on, Alan and his fellow codebreakers complained that they didn't have enough resources – including typists, translators and unskilled staff – to help them break the code. But their complaints weren't listened to and they were told to make do with what they had.

They went over the heads of their superiors and wrote to the ***prime minister***, Winston Churchill. A man named Stuart Milner-Barry – who worked in Hut 6 – took the train to London and ***delivered the letter*** to Winston Churchill at 10 Downing Street by hand.

Winston Churchill wrote in his notes for that day:

'MAKE SURE *they have all they want on* EXTREME PRIORITY *and report to me that this* HAS BEEN DONE.'

Did You Know?

During the war over two hundred bombes were built. In case any were damaged in an attack they were spread between Bletchley Park and its outstations in Wavendon, Adstock and Gayhurst in Buckinghamshire, and Eastcote and Stanmore in Middlesex.

The intelligence gathered by Alan and his team of codebreakers was *crucial* in the efforts to stop the war. Coordinates gathered via the bombe helped the Allies avoid German U-boats during the *Battle of the Atlantic*.

Alan the eccentric

While working at Bletchley Park, Alan lodged at the Crown Inn in the village of Shenley Brook End. Alan suffered from terrible **hay fever** and would cycle to work wearing a **gas mask** to avoid the effects of the pollen.

The chain on his bicycle would come off regularly. Instead of having it mended he would count the number of times the pedals went around in order to stop the chain from coming loose. He even devised a mathematical formula for when this would happen.

DID YOU KNOW?
Alan's colleagues called him 'Prof', and his notes on the Enigma code were known as 'The Prof's Book'. He chained his mug to the radiator pipes to stop it from being stolen!

Alan was a talented **long-distance runner**, occasionally running the forty miles to London when he was needed for top-secret meetings. He once tried out for the British Olympic team, although his hopes were hampered by an injury.

Silver bars

During the war, when it seemed like a German invasion was IMMINENT, Alan devised a hare-brained scheme to **protect his savings**. He converted some of his money into silver bars, loaded them into an old pram and headed off into the woods near Shenley to bury them.

> IMMINENT: when something is imminent it is about to happen.

Alan meant to go back and find the silver bars when the war was over – but by the time he went back he had completely forgotten where they were! The silver bars remain missing to this day.

Joan Clarke

One of Alan's best friends at Bletchley Park was a woman named Joan Clarke, a fellow **codebreaker** who worked with him in Hut 8.

Joan and Alan had met before when they were both students at Cambridge University. It was one of Joan's lecturers at Cambridge who had recommended her for the job at Bletchley Park.

Joan was supposed to work in Hut 6 on translation, as she could speak fluent German. However, when they found out she was so good at **maths** she was moved to Hut 8 to work with Alan and his colleagues.

While they were at Bletchley Park, they would go cycling and take walks and trips to the cinema together. Joan and Alan were **intellectual equals**, and Joan liked that Alan treated her with respect. Women at Bletchley Park were **paid less** than men, even though they did the same job.

In 1941 Alan proposed to Joan and they were engaged for six months. Then Alan told Joan he was gay, and they called off the marriage. Joan wasn't fazed at all, and they remained friends for many years.

Life after the war

Alan was appointed an Officer of the Order of the British Empire (OBE) by King George VI in 1945. However, due to the top-secret nature of Alan's work, many people didn't find out about it until long after he died.

Top-secret work

Mavis Lever was a codebreaker at Bletchley Park. While she was there she met another codebreaker called Keith Batey. The two of them married in 1942. They were put on different sections at Bletchley Park and forbidden from talking about their work – in fact, it was so secret that Mavis didn't find out what her husband had been working on until after he had died and the Bletchley Park documents were DECLASSIFIED.

DECLASSIFIED: no longer top secret – open to the public.

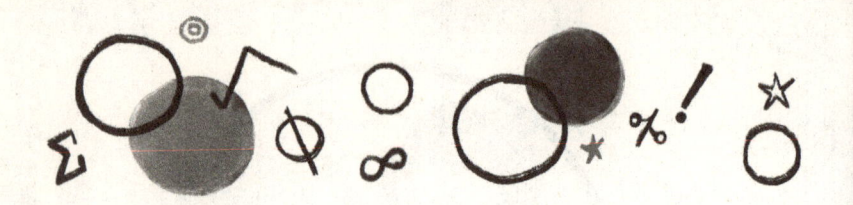

After the war Alan worked at the National Physical Laboratory in Teddington in London.

Alan had already come up with the idea for the modern computer when he invented the Turing machine in 1936. At Bletchley Park he had seen special machines – including the bombe and the COLOSSUS – organized to do different tasks. Now Alan wanted to put the two ideas together and create a ***single programmable machine*** that could do any task asked of it – essentially a computer.

COLOSSUS: another codebreaking machine.

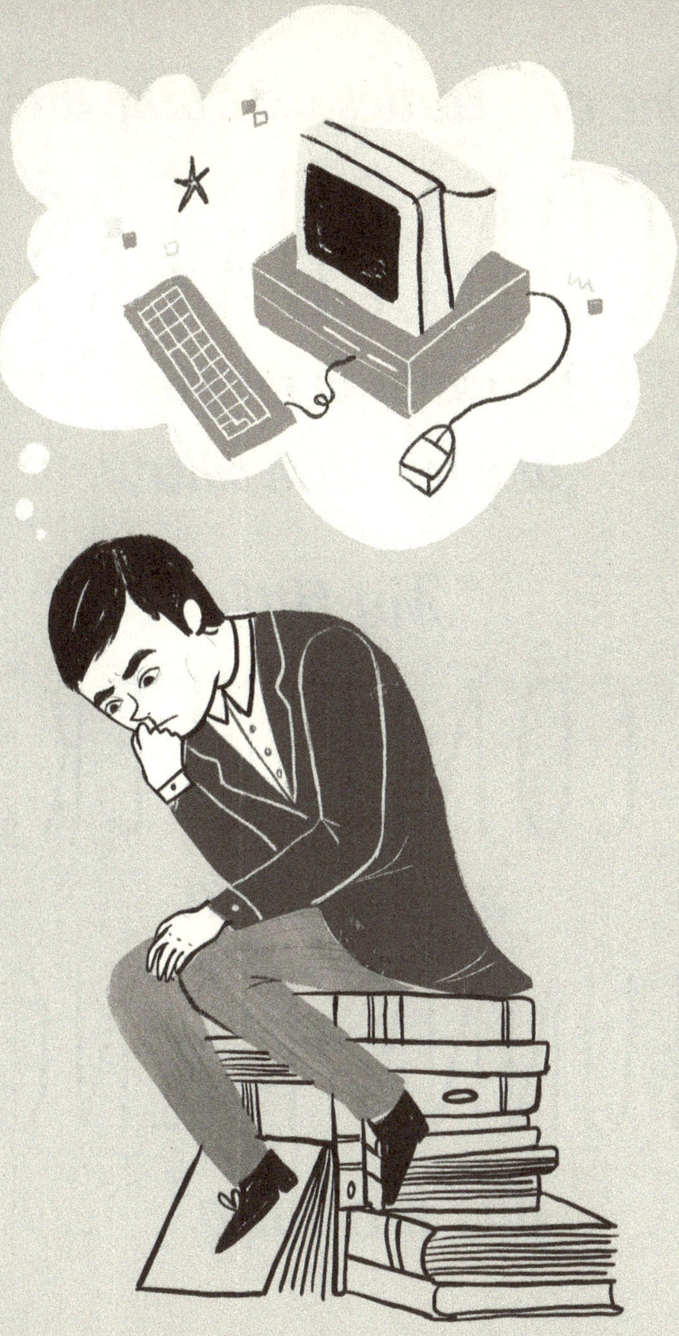

'One day ladies will take their COMPUTERS for walks in the park and tell each other, "My little COMPUTER said such a FUNNY THING this morning".'

At the National Physical Laboratory Alan taught himself **electronics** so he could put his theories into practice. In 1945 he put forward his idea for an 'electronic brain' called ACE, or Automatic Computing Engine, which was accepted.

Whereas a lot of the early computers were based on numbers and arithmetic, Alan's computer would work with **symbols of any kind.** However, the amount of storage Alan's computer would have needed to work – about six kilobytes in today's language – was considered too expensive, so the project stalled and Alan resigned.

Alan knew his machine would work because of his war experience with similar devices but couldn't say so because it was secret. His coworkers didn't believe such a machine was possible, let alone affordable.

Alan's ACE wouldn't be built until 1950, when his colleagues used a scaled-back version of his original plan to build the 'Pilot ACE', the fastest working computer at the time.

Alan moved to Manchester in 1948, where he was appointed as Deputy Director of the Computing Machine Laboratory at Manchester University a year later. There Alan would get to work on some of the world's *first working computers*, which were known as the Manchester computers. Alan would have worked on the Manchester Mark 1.

These huge computers took up whole rooms and used large 'tubes' – known as Williams tubes or Williams-Kilburn tubes after their inventors Frederic Williams and Tom Kilburn – to store data. Each tube stored only 1,024 'bits' of data – a tiny amount!

The first computer programs calculated large numbers. Alan wrote a program that did long division.

'PROGRAMMING *is a skill* BEST *acquired by* PRACTICE *and* EXAMPLE *rather than from books.*'

Did You Know?

In 1946 Alan proposed that it would be possible to link his ACE computer so it could be operated REMOTELY via telephone cable - basically doing what the internet does before it had even been invented!

REMOTE: from a distance, without physical contact.

Artificial intelligence

Later in his life Alan turned his attention to artificial intelligence, a field so new that it hadn't even been named yet!

In 1950 Alan devised the Turing test, which determines a machine's ability to trick someone into believing it is human.

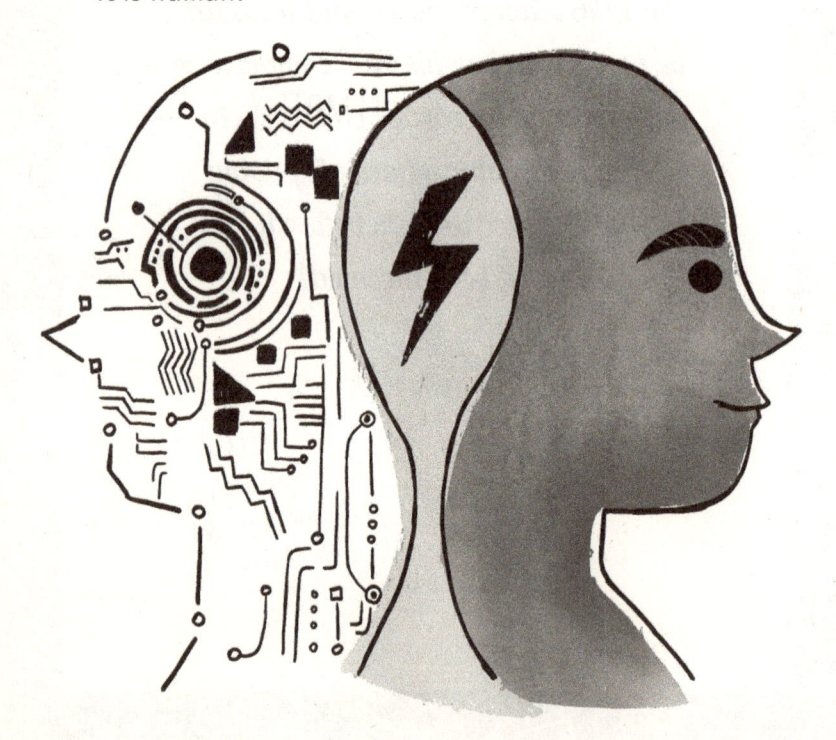

'I propose to consider THE QUESTION, "Can MACHINES think?".'

'A COMPUTER would deserve to be called INTELLIGENT if it could deceive a HUMAN into BELIEVING that it was human.'

Alan proposed an 'imitation game' where a judge would sit behind a screen, having a text-only conversation with two partners. One of the partners would be a real person, the other a computer. The judge would have to figure out which was the real person.

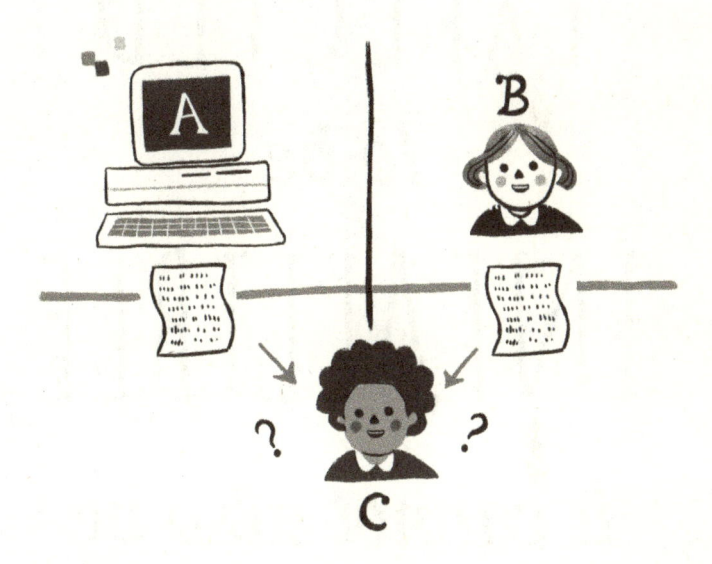

If the judge couldn't tell which of the partners was the real person, the computer would have 'passed' the test.

The computer is judged on how closely its answers *resemble* those a real person would give, so it doesn't need to give correct answers – in fact, it might be better that it sometimes doesn't!

'*If a machine is* EXPECTED *to be* INFALLIBLE, *it cannot also be* INTELLIGENT.'

Alan was excited by the idea of machines that could think – his friend Robin Gandy talked about him reading from his 'Turing test' papers with a smile and a giggle.

The imitation game today

The Loebner Prize is an annual competition where artificial intelligence bots play Alan's original imitation game and are judged on how 'human-like' they are, with the winner receiving a cash prize and a bronze medal. There's an even better prize, though: $100,000 and a gold medal, to be awarded to the first computer whose responses are completely INDISTINGUISHABLE from a human's. This prize has never been won.

INDISTINGUISHABLE: unable to tell apart.

LOEBNER PRIZE

"Can machines think?"
Alan M. Turing

'I believe that at the end of the century the use of words and GENERAL EDUCATED OPINION will have altered so much that one will be able to SPEAK of MACHINES thinking without expecting to be CONTRADICTED.'

Persecution

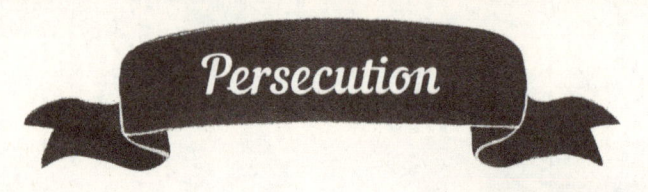

$\mathcal{A}$lan was PERSECUTED during his lifetime for being gay.

PERSECUTION: oppression or ill treatment against someone, particularly based on factors like their race, gender or sexual orientation.

NEW THEORY CLAIMS
HOMOSEXUALITY CAN BE CURED

400 MORE HOMOSEXUALS OUSTED FROM GOV'T JOBS

In 1951 Alan met a man named Arnold Murray outside the Regal Cinema, in Manchester where they both lived. He invited him to lunch. Alan and Arnold got along well, so they began a ***relationship***.

But then Alan believed that Arnold stole £10 from Alan's wallet. Though Arnold tried to convince Alan he hadn't, Alan broke off the relationship.

The next year, Alan's home was **burgled**. The burglar took a shirt, some knives, a pair of trousers, shoes, razors, a compass and an open bottle of sherry. Arnold was the prime suspect.

Arnold turned up at Alan's house to convince him he was innocent. He told Alan he thought it was someone else that he knew called Harry.

When the police investigated the burglary they found Harry's fingerprints in Alan's home. Arnold had been telling the **truth**. However, now the police were suspicious about Alan and Arnold's relationship.

When the police questioned him about how he knew Arnold, Alan nervously blurted out the truth. At the time being gay was *illegal*, so Alan was arrested and *convicted*.

Alan's lawyers defended him, saying he was a **national asset** for the work he had done developing the computer. They also used the OBE he was awarded for services during the war to back up their case. But since the incredible work Alan had done at Bletchley Park and Hut 8 was still considered **top secret**, it was not able to be used as evidence.

Since Alan had been arrested and convicted, he was branded a **security risk** and was no longer able to work as a programmer. He was given a choice between **prison** and a **chemical treatment** that was supposed to stop him from being attracted to men.

Alan chose the treatment. It was a hormonal treatment that was TRAUMATIC for Alan's body and mind, and of course it didn't change his sexuality at all.

> TRAUMATIC: deeply disturbing or distressing.

The treatment, as well as the harsh conviction and the fact that he was no longer able to do the job he loved, meant Alan fell into a deep depression.

Alan was worried that people would use his homosexuality to discount the incredible work he had done in computer science and artificial intelligence.

Alan's death

*I*n 1954 Alan's housekeeper found him dead from cyanide poisoning.

Some people believe that Alan poisoned himself. He was found with a half-eaten apple by his bed, which may have been the way he consumed the fatal dose. Others believe it was the result of an experiment gone wrong.

Alan was cremated at Woking Crematorium on 12 June 1954.

Did You Know?

The Apple logo - an apple with a bite taken out of it - which you can see on the back of an iPhone or an Apple computer is often mistakenly linked to Alan Turing, as a tribute to 'the grandfather of the modern computer' and the apple that killed him. However, the original designer of the logo, Rob Janoff, has said that it was inspired by Sir Isaac Newton, who discovered gravity.

Pardon

In 2009 over thirty thousand people signed a petition asking the British government to issue a public apology for the terrible and traumatic way Alan had been treated towards the end of his life, just for being gay.

Gordon Brown, who was prime minister at the time, issued the apology, saying that Alan's treatment had been utterly unfair and that he and the government were deeply sorry. Later Queen Elizabeth II granted Alan an official pardon for his conviction.

'ALAN and the thousands of other GAY MEN who were CONVICTED, as he was convicted, under HOMOPHOBIC LAWS, were treated TERRIBLY.'

– Gordon Brown

A 2017 law that pardons anyone who was convicted for being gay in the past is affectionately known as the *Alan Turing law*. Almost fifty thousand men have been pardoned since the law was introduced.

Did You Know?

ALAN TURING
1912-1954
CODEBREAKER
lived here
from
1945-1947

Blue plaques are placed on buildings where people of note lived, died or did important things. Alan has lots of blue plaques all around England. In Maida Vale and St Leonards-on-Sea, where he grew up; at Sherborne, where he went to school; at King's College, Cambridge, where he went to university; at the University of Manchester, where he worked towards the end of his life; and in Wilmslow, where he died.

'Without his OUTSTANDING CONTRIBUTION, the history of the SECOND WORLD WAR could have been very different. He truly was one of those individuals . . . whose UNIQUE CONTRIBUTION helped to turn the tide of war.'

– Gordon Brown

At Bletchley Park, where Alan helped invent the bombe, there is a special Engineering Heritage Award plaque.

The plaque commemorating the place in Maida Vale where Alan was born was replaced with a ***rainbow plaque*** in 2017 to celebrate Pride in London, as part of a special project honouring notable LGBTQ+ people who lived and worked in the city.

LGBTQ+: is a term for someone who identifies as lesbian, gay, bisexual, transgender, queer or many other terms denoted by '+'.

ALAN TURING
Code Breaker & Pioneer of Computer Science
LOVE LIVED HERE
1912-1954

Tributes

Alan has been honoured in many different ways since his death.

Universities all over the world – including the University of Manchester – have buildings named after him. The computer room at King's College, Cambridge, where Alan went to university, is called the Turing Room.

In Manchester there is also an Alan Turing Way and an Alan Turing Bridge.

A film about Alan's life was made in 2014. It was called *The Imitation Game* and starred Benedict Cumberbatch, and was nominated for several Oscars.

Did You Know?

Board game company Hasbro released an 'Alan Turing' version of Monopoly. The special edition was based on a hand-drawn version of the game Alan played when he was at Bletchley Park. It featured huts and blocks instead of houses and hotels, and included landmarks that were important in Alan's life, such as Maida Vale and Hut 8. Alan's face is on all the banknotes. The special edition was sold to raise money to help renovate and refurbish Bletchley Park, which has since opened as a museum.

Perhaps the Monopoly money foretold the future. In 2019 it was announced Alan's face would be a feature of the new £50 note, in celebration of his achievements.

Statue

A bronze statue of Alan now sits on a bench in Manchester. The bench includes the motto 'IEKYF RQMSI ADXUO KVKZC GUBJ' – the phrase 'Founder of Computer Science', written in code.

You might remember from page 62 that a letter from a coded phrase cannot match its encryption. Can you see a letter in the encrypted motto that is in the same position as the coded phrase?

Timeline

1912
Alan Mathison Turing is born in Maida Vale, London.

1926
Alan goes to Sherborne and becomes very interested in science and maths.

1928
Alan meets Christopher Morcom.

1930
Christopher Morcom dies tragically at the age of eighteen.

1931
Alan attends King's College in Cambridge to study maths.

1934
Alan graduates from King's College with top marks.

1936
Alan invites the Turing Machine.

1939

The Second World War is declared. Alan arrives at Bletchley Park to work as a codebreaker.

1940

Alan helps develop the bombe, a device for breaking the Enigma code.

1945

Alan is awarded an OBE for his services during the war.

1950

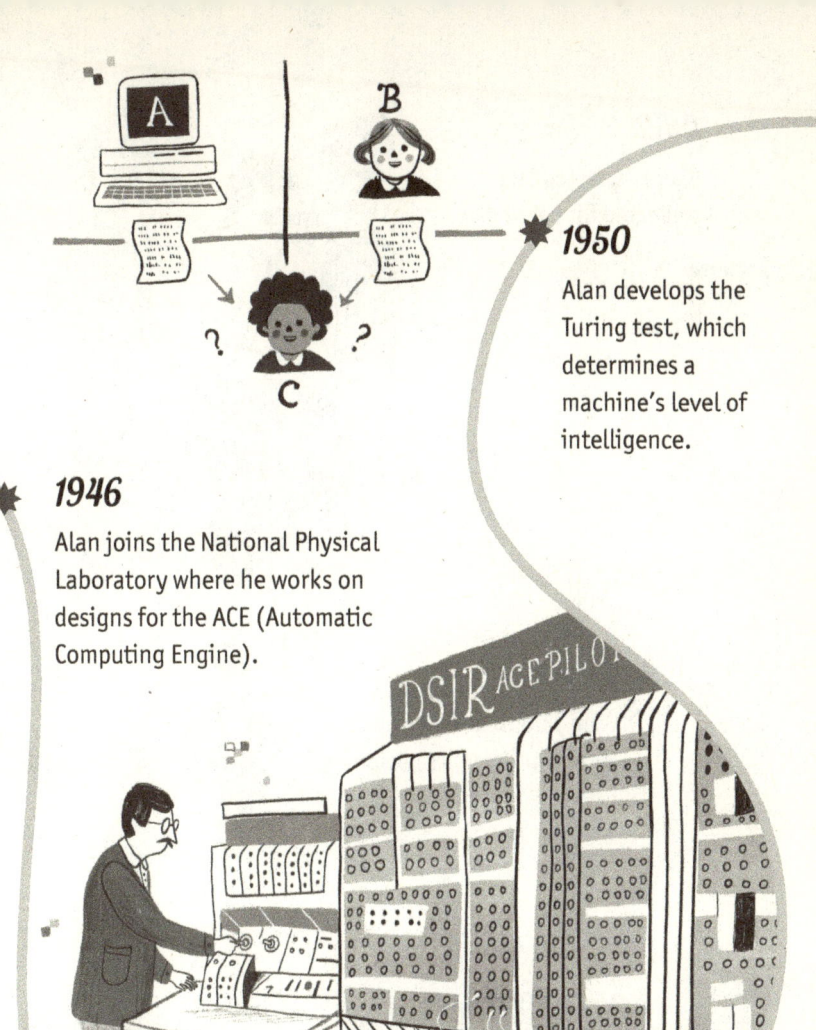

Alan develops the Turing test, which determines a machine's level of intelligence.

1946

Alan joins the National Physical Laboratory where he works on designs for the ACE (Automatic Computing Engine).

1948

Alan starts working at Manchester University.

1952
Alan is arrested and convicted for being gay.

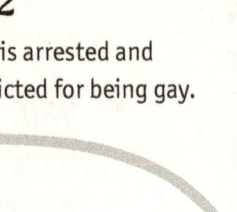

1954
Alan's housekeeper finds him dead from cyanide poisoning.

2001
A statue of Alan is unveiled in Sackville Gardens, Manchester.

2019

Bank of England announces Alan Turing will be the face of the £50 note.

2017

A law that pardons men who were convicted for being gay in the past is passed, and is affectionately known as the 'Alan Turing law'.

2009

Alan receives a posthumous (awarded after death) pardon from the government.

2013

Alan receives a posthumous pardon from Queen Elizabeth II.

Index

artificial intelligence 4, 9, 90–97
Atkins, James 47

Batey, Keith 79
Bletchley Park 4, 59–69, 79, 110
Brewster, Edwin Tenney 15
Brown, Gordon 106, 107, 109

Cambridge University 38–9, 44–7, 53, 55–56, 111
Chamberlain, Neville 58
Churchill, Winston 66–67
Clarke, Joan 74–77
computers 80, 82–89
    bombe 4, 9, 62–65
    Turing machine 1, 3, 9, 47, 48–51

Einstein, Albert 31–32
Enigma machine 60–65

Lever, Mavis 79

Manchester University 86–87, 111
Morcom, Christopher 34–43
Morcom, Frances Isobel 40
Murray, Arnold 99–101

Newton, Sir Isaac 31, 33, 105

Second World War 58, 59
    codebreaking 1, 4, 59–69, 78–79

Sherborne 26–36

Turing, Alan
    artificial intelligence 4, 9, 90–97
    and autism 43
    bombe 4, 9, 62–65, 68–69
    Cambridge University 3, 38–39, 44–47, 53, 55–56
    and Christopher Morcom 34–42
    codebreaking 1, 4, 7, 57, 59–69, 113
    computers 80, 82–9
    death 6, 104
    early life 1, 2, 10–15
    eccentricity 70–73
    as a gay man 6, 47, 98–103
    in Germany 53–54
    growing up 17–25
    and Joan Clarke 74–77
    life after the war 78–89
    pardon 106–108
    plaques 108, 110
    Sherborne 26–36
    statue 113
    timeline 114–119
    tributes 105, 111–113
Turing machine 1, 3, 9, 47, 48–51
Turing test 4, 9, 90–97

Williams, Denis 53–54

Quote Sources

Direct quotes throughout are from *Alan Turing: The Enigma* (Andrew Hodges, Vintage, 1992) except the below:

Pages 5, 91, 92, 97: Turing, A. M., 'Computing Machinery and Intelligence', *Mind: A Quarterly Review of Psychology and Philosophy*, Volume 59, No. 236 (1950)

Pages 8, 16, 94: Copeland, B. J., *The Essential Turing*, Oxford University Press, Oxford, 2004

Page 21: 'Alan Turing: The father of modern computing credited with saving millions of lives' (Colin Drury, *Independent*, 2019)

Pages 25, 40: *Unpublished writings of A. M. Turing* © The Provost and Scholars of Kings College Cambridge, 2020

Pages 45: Horizon: *The Strange Life and Death of Dr Turing* (1992). BBC: https://www.youtube.com/watch?v=Z-sTs2o0VuY

Page 52: Turing, A. M., 'Intelligent Machinery: A Report by A. M. Turing', submitted to the National Physical Laboratory (1948)

Page 58: 'Neville Chamberlain's declaration of war' (As transcribed for the *Guardian*, 2009)

Page 88: Cooper, S. B. and J. van Leeuwen (eds), *Alan Turing: His Work and Impact*, Elsevier, Waltham, MA, 2013

Pages 107, 109: https://blog.jgc.org/2011/07/complete-text-of-gordon-browns-apology.html

Have you read about all of these extraordinary people?

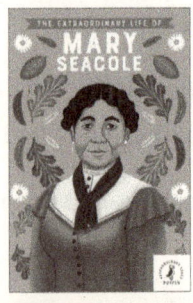

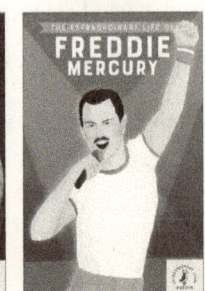

- Stephen Hawking
- Michelle Obama
- Malala Yousafzai
- Anne Frank
- Katherine Johnson
- Neil Armstrong
- Mary Seacole
- Rosa Parks
- Mahatma Gandhi
- Greta Thunberg
- Freddie Mercury
- Serena Williams